Container Flower Gardening:

Guide of Annuals for Balcony Garden

How to Select, Grow and Take Care of Annuals for Beginners

Light ▪ Hardiness ▪ Size ▪ Color ▪ Soil ▪ Time of Blooming

Katherine Legrand

Table of Contents

Introduction

The tradition of decorating our houses with plants was started a long time ago. In the beginning, only herbs were cultivated indoor, but then some beautifully flowering plants were added to them.

Decorative plants in your apartment or on your balcony are a part of nature right next to you. A few well-chosen plants create a pleasant atmosphere and make your house the coziest place in the world.

With the help of decorative containers, various suspension system and supports, you can create a lot of original compositions, which will transform the interior of your apartment.

You can practice flower growing not only on a balcony or a terrace. You can also use windowsills. In addition to your apartment, you can decorate your workplace in your office.

This book was written for people who are in love with flowers and for those who want to find a fascinating hobby as well.

If you want to create a flourishing area at home, you need to know the rules of growing plants, have an idea of what conditions are necessary for one or another flower. All this information you will find in this book.

In the firsts chapters, you will discover the guide to annual flowers:

▪ All the plants are divided into groups according to their light conditions (shade, part shade, full sun), temperature (hardy, half-hardy, tender), color and height, germination temperature, time to bloom and duration of blooming. With this information, you can easy understand which flowers are more suitable for your place.

• Also you will learn how to work with other annuals which are not included in this book (there are thousands of annuals, so it's impossible to describe all in one book).

Then we talk about seeds and seedlings. The last chapter is devoted to a new one in flower gardening. In this section, I will show how to do all the process step-by-step from choosing an idea to realizing it in life.

Let's not waste time on a long preface, let's start immediately.

1. Life Forms of Annual Plants

There are many types of flowering plants. The most frequently used forms for balcony, patio and terrace landscaping are vines and climbers, hanging plants, and, of course, annual and perennial herbaceous plants. Sometimes you can use bulbs as well.

I am going to use a word "balcony" here and further, please, keep in mind that you can grow flowers wherever you like: any place as a terrace, patio, roof or windowsill are suitable for this.

In this book, we are going to talk mainly about different annuals, but some attention will be paid to other types.

1.1. Vines

These plants have long and flexible stems. They are very decorative. Vines can be used for vertical landscaping and as ground covers as well.

They grow very fast and can be combined with different inert materials, such as ceramic, wood, stone or metal. Also they can be united with other plants.

The suitable vines (climbers) for indoor flower gardening and balcony gardening as well:

• Flowering: Morning Glory, Sweat peas, Trumpet creeper (Campsis radicans), Clematis, Hoya, Cissus, Clockvine

5

(Thunbergia), Climbing Hydrangea, Honeysuckle, Passion flower (Passiflora), Climbing Rose, Moonflower, Snail vine.

▪ Non-flowering: Asparagus benuissimus, Ivy (Hedera), Virginia creeper (Parthenocissus quinquefolia), hops.

1.2. Hanging plants

Hanging plants are rarely named as ampel. The name "ample" comes from German. "Ampel" means "hanging basket". Ampel plants are planted in hanging containers so their stems hang down.

Usually we grow hanging plants in regular pots and containers, but also we can buy plant hangers. Today there is a big offer in on-line shops. You can buy plant hangers of any form and any size.

Ampel plants can be used as single or be planted around big plants at the borders of the pot.

Flowering: ampel Petunia, Begonia, Fuchsia, Jasmine, Geranium (Pelargonium), Lobelia, Water hyssop (Bacopa monnieri), Nasturtium.

Non-flowering: Tradescantia, Dichondra.

1.3. Bulbs

You know that the majority of bulbs bloom in spring. So you can use them only at this time. They need some special care after the blooming end and, as for me, they are middle-hard for growing.

I can't recommend bulbs for beginners. The difficulty is not with the growing complexity. It is in the further care of the bulbs and their storage.

Flowering: Tulip, Daffodil, Crocus, Hippeastrum, Haemanthus, and Crinum.

1.4. Woody plants

There we talk about small bushes and trees. You can grow at your home any plant you want, but you have to pay attention to growing speed of a plant. It's very reasonable to choose slow-growing dwarf forms for indoor gardening.

Flowering: Indian mallow (Abutilon), Oleander, Wisteria.

Non-flowering: Juniperus, Thujopsis.

1.5. Herbaceous plants

Herbaceous plants are very numerous. You can plant them anywhere you like. You know that herbaceous plants can be annual or perennial. The first ones live only one year; the second ones live two or more years.

A biennial plant is a flowering plant that takes two years to complete its biological life cycle. In the first year, a plant grows leaves, stems, and roots (vegetative structures), then it enters a period of dormancy over the colder months. Perennials live and bloom more than two years.

In the balcony gardening, you can use both types of plants flowering and non-flowering. Non-flowering plants usually are used as the background for flowering ones.

You should use perennials and woody plants for balcony gardening only if you can take them indoor in winter. If you don't have enough space in your apartment, use annuals only. But there are a few exceptions If you can cover them very well in winter, you can grow almost everything you want.

For a sunny balcony, I recommend from the perennials Arabis, Iberis, Iris, Rockfoils (Saxifraga). Also, if your space allows, you can grow Clematis and Hydrangea.

For non-sunny terraces, you can use Aquilegia, Fuchsia, Dicentra, Astilbe. From woody vines – Virginia creeper (Parthenocissus).

2. Guide of Annual Herbaceous Flowers

When we choose flowers, we should consider their height, time of blooming, color and growth character. About the last one we have already talked. Plants can be climbing, hanging or normal growing.

Along with above-listed ratings the great importance is paid for the fragrance of flowers. The most fragrant flowers are Alyssum, Reseda, Nicotiana, Sweet peas.

2.1. How to use the guide

You can find some tips and advice on how to use this guide in Chapter 3. Therefore, I say just a few words here.

Next classification will help you to select the most appropriate plants for your conditions. At first, you should figure out what is an orientation of your balcony. According to that you can start picking up the plants.

Some people may have troubles with the definition of the orientation. I can suggest a simple and modern way without using a compass (I suppose that not so many people have a compass at home).

You can use www. maps.google.com where you will find your house location. Zoom in the map and determine the orientation of your balcony. Remember, on the Google maps the north is on the top, the south is on the bottom, the east is on the right and the west is on the left. It's easy.

You need to find only a relative orientation. For example, you see your balcony between the north and west (not directly). It means that you can choose plants suitable for the north and the west together.

2.2. Lighting conditions

All plants need sunlight for the process of photosynthesis. During photosynthesis plants use the energy of sunlight, water, and carbon dioxide to create glucose (sugar). A plant for energy can later utilize the glucose. Also, our plants need sunlight to grow green.

The right amount of sunlight required for annual flowers varies. It depends on species, thus, we can find annuals suitable for shade, partial shade or full sun areas.

Full shade or deep shade means that no direct sunlight reaches the ground. We can find this on the north sides of buildings.

Part shade or part sun areas exist on the east and west side of buildings. Plants growing there receive the direct morning or afternoon sunlight.

Full sun places (on the south side) are given direct sunlight for at least 6 hours or more each day, including all or some of the midday hours.

The difference between these plants is that full shade plants need only a few hours of light a day while full sun plants need eight or more hours of light a day.

Shade annuals: Balsam, China aster, Coleus, Impatiens, Polka dot plant, Torenia.

Part shade annuals: Ageratum, Alyssum, Balsam, Cleome, Coleus, Cosmos, Dichondra, Impatiens, Lobelia, Marigold, Nasturtium, Pansy, Petunia, Polka dot plant, Portulaca, Snapdragon, Sweet peas, Torenia, Verbena.

Full sun annuals: Ageratum, Alyssum, Balsam, Cleome, Coleus, Cosmos, Dichondra, Gomphrena, Lobelia, Marigold, Morning Glory, Pansy, Petunia, Portulaca, Nasturtium, Snapdragon, Sunflower, Sweet peas, Verbena, Zinnia

Warning!

On hot summer days, even flowers for a full sun area may suffer from direct sunlight and feel the lack of moistening. You should protect them from the direct light on these days if you want them to be healthy and good-looking.

2.3. Hardiness

Hardy

Hardy annual seeds can handle being frozen in the soil and are often planted in fall or early spring. A lot of self-seeding annuals would be considered hardy seeds.

For example, Alyssum, Viola, Dianthus. Hardy annuals (the abbreviation HA in seed catalogs) tolerate light frosts.

Half-hardy

Half-hardy seeds can be direct sown after all danger of frost. They don't like being frozen in the ground, but don't need to wait until the soil warms.

Sometimes it's just easier to start these seeds indoors and move them out as plants. Examples of half-hardy annuals include Cosmos, Gazania and Petunia.

Half-hardy annual plants can survive a couple of days with the night temperatures 35 - 45 degrees F (1-7 °C) and a light frost, but anything colder will turn them to death.

Just like hardy annuals, the longer they get used to the changing temperature, the harder they become.

Tender (cold-sensible)

Most so-called tender annuals are tropical perennials. Tender annuals would include Begonia, Impatiens and Zinnia.

Tender annual seeds must not be planted outdoors until the soil warms and the temperatures are reliably well above freezing at night. Cold-sensible annuals can't handle anything colder than about 55 degrees F (12 °C).

Hardy: Alyssum, Lobelia, Pansy.

Half-hardy: Cleome, Marigold, Morning Glory, Nasturtium, Petunia, Snapdragon, Sweet peas, Sunflower.

Tender: Ageratum, Balsam, China aster, Coleus, Cosmos, Dichondra, Gomphrena, Impatiens, Polka dot plant, Portulaca, Torenia, Verbena, Zinnia.

Hardiness to the balcony gardening has only one purpose. You have to know when you can carry out your plants on your balcony. Hardy annuals can be planted directly outside. Half-hardy and tender ones should be sown indoor and then depending on the weather conditions carry out on your balcony.

2.4. Types of soils

There are a lot of types of soils that gardeners usually work with.

<u>Clay soil</u> is the heaviest and densest form. This soil retains and holds large amounts of nutrients and water, but makes hard for air to penetrate it.

<u>Silty soil</u> retains plenty of water, but the lack of nutrients comparing to other types.

<u>Sandy soil</u> is considered one of the worst. It keeps the water very badly. It is hard for the plant roots to establish on it.

<u>Chalky soil</u> is not an ideal soil for plants. It has low water content with high lime content, so its pH level of 7.5 – alkali.

<u>Peaty soil</u> has a lot of organic materials and rich of water. This soil is very good for plants but it needs to be drained. The pH level of peaty soil is a little acidic.

<u>Loamy soil</u> is the perfect type because it is a mix of clay, silt, sand and some humus. It has high calcium level and can retain water and nutrients very well. Also it is well aerated. Its pH level is 6-7 – neutral.

For the majority of annuals, you can use regular potting soil. It can be organic or mixed, but usually, it means loamy soil. You can buy it anywhere – in every shop including on-line ones.

2.5. Watering

Our plants always need water. How often you should water them depends on how much water a particular flower needs.

Low watering: Cleome, Dichondra, Marigold, Nasturtium, Portulaca, Sunflower, Zinnia.

Average watering: Ageratum, Alyssum, China aster, Cosmos, Gomphrena, Morning Glory, Pansy, Petunia, Polka dot plant, Snapdragon, Sweet peas, Verbena.

High watering (this means that the soil should always be wet, but not sloppy): Balsam (likes spraying too), Coleus (likes spraying too), Impatiens, Lobelia, Torenia.

According to this, it is not reasonable to plant together low watering plants and those which prefer the moist soil.

2.6. Germination temperature

59-65 degree F (15-18 °C): Ageratum, Morning Glory, Nasturtium, Sunflower (can germinate even in less temperature)

65-70 degree F (18-21 °C): Alyssum, Balsam, China aster, Lobelia, Marigold, Pansy, Snapdragon, Sweet peas, Torenia, Verbena.

70-77 degree F (21-25 °C): Cleome, Coleus, Cosmos, Dichondra (sow seeds in February), Impatiens, Gomphrena, Petunia, Polka dot plant, Portulaca, Zinnia.

Seeds have a temperature range within which they germinate. They will not do so above or below this range.

Here we talk about the temperature of the soil first of all. If the temperature in your apartment is cooler than needed, you can set your trays on the heater for a few houses.

Also, you can use warm or even hot water. In the case when the temperature is higher than a maximum, you can open the window in the room for some time.

2.7. Days from germination to bloom

We might read such information in the many books and web pages: indoor sowing 4 to 6 weeks before the last frost.

This common phrase to my mind is useless. I don't know anyone who can predict the weather for more than three days. So how can we find out when the last frost will be?

By the way, nowadays Earth's climate is changing notably fast from year to year, and we can't rely very much on the last year weather.

That's why it is important to know the time needed for a plant to germinate and to bloom. Knowing that allows us to calculate the date for seed sowing.

For example:

We know that our plant gives flowers in June. The period to germinate is 7 days and time to bloom is at least 60 days.

When should we start seeds?

60 days for maturing plus 7 days for germination – 67 days in all.

So to receive blooming in the middle June we should start our seeds at the beginning of April.

I know it is not the accurate calculation, but it works. For reliability, you can add 5-7 extra days.

Days to germinate:

3-7 days: Ageratum, Morning Glory, Sunflower, Sweet peas, Zinnia.

7-14 days: China aster, Cleome, Coleus, Cosmos, Dichondra, Marigold, Nasturtium, Petunia, Polka dot plant, Portulaca, Snapdragon, Torenia.

14 days and more: Alyssum, Balsam, Impatiens, Gomphrena, Lobelia, Pansy, Verbena.

Days to bloom after germination:

40-60 days: Nasturtium.

60-80 days: Ageratum, Alyssum, China aster, Cleome, Cosmos, Gomphrena, Marigold, Morning Glory, Petunia, Portulaca, dwarf Snapdragon, Sunflower, Sweet peas, Zinnia.

80-100 days: Balsam, Impatiens, Lobelia, Pansy, tall Snapdragon, Torenia, Verbena.

2.8. Time of blooming

The majority of annuals give blooming in summer.

Summer: Ageratum (June-August), Alyssum (June-October), Balsam (June-September), Cleome (June-September), Cosmos (end June-August), Gomphrena (June-July-October), Impatiens (May-October), Lobelia (June-September), Marigold (June-September), Morning Glory (June-September), Nasturtium (June-September), Pansy (May-August), Petunia (June-September), Portulaca (July-September), Snapdragon (June-July-October), Sunflower (June-July), Sweet peas (July-September), Torenia (June-August), Verbena (July-September), Zinnia (May-September).

Fall: China aster (August-October).

2.9. Color

Red, orange, yellow: Marigold, Nasturtium, Sunflower, Zinnia.

Blue, violet: Ageratum, Lobelia.

Multiple: Alyssum (white, pink, purple, yellow), Balsam (yellow, red, orange, violet, pink, white), China aster (white, pink, violet, red), Cleome (white, pink, lavender), Cosmos (white, pink, violet), Gomphrena (pink, violet, purple, red), Impatiens (bi-color, red, orange, yellow, pink, salmon, white), Morning Glory (bi-color, pure, striped, various),

Pansy (bi-color, various), Petunia (various), Portulaca (orange, pink, red, white, yellow), Snapdragon (various), Sweet peas (various), Torenia (bi-color, white, yellow, pink, violet), Verbena (white, red, pink, violet).

Harmonious combinations are always pleasant for eyes. These can be:

▪ Monochromatic planting (one-color);

▪ 2-3 close tones (light pink, pink, rose-red; white, light purple, light pink);

▪ Contrast (orange and blue, yellow and violet or purple).

White flowers can neutralize disharmony of combinations. They reduce cool colors and increase warm ones.

Plant for background without flowers: Coleus, Dichondra, Polka dot plant.

2.10. Height

Small 4-12 inches (10-30 cm): Ageratum, Alyssum, Coleus, Lobelia, Pansy, Petunia, Portulaca, dwarf Snapdragon, Torenia.

Medium 12-20 inches (30-50 cm): Balsam, China aster, Coleus, Cosmos, Gomphrena, Impatiens, Marigold, Nasturtium, Snapdragon, Sunflower, Verbena, Zinnia.

Tall more than 20 inches (50 cm): Cleome, Cosmos, Dichondra, Polka dot plant, Marigold, Morning Glory, Snapdragon (tall varieties), Sunflower, Sweet peas, Zinnia.

2.11. List of flowers

The first name of the plant is the name used in this book. Its Latin name is given in brackets, and then common names are listed.

- **Ageratum** (Ageratum mexicanum, Ageratum houstonianum). Modern varieties are "Adriatic" (Floss flower), "Blue Mink", "Blue Danube", and "Hawaii".

Sow seeds in the same container where the plants will grow all the time because ageratum may not survive transplanting.

The spacing between plants should be 5-6 inches (10-15 cm).

- **Alyssum** (Lobularia maritima is very close to it), also known as Sweet Alyssum.

During propagation cut stems on 2-3 inches (5-8 cm) that stimulate new growing and new blooming.

The spacing between plants should be 5 inches (10-12 cm).

- **Balsam** (Impatiens balsamina), also known as Touch-Me-Not, Garden Balsam, Rose Balsam. Heirloom plant.

The spacing between plants should be 10-12 inches (25-30 cm). Don't use this plant on a windy balcony, or protect it from the drought.

- **China aster** (Callistephus chinensis). Seeds are started in early May. Seedlings are transplanted outside at the end of May.

Flowers of China aster look like the full suns. You can use a potassium fertilizer before the blooming starts.

The distance between plants should be 7-10 inches (20-30 cm).

1. Balsam 2. Alyssum 3. Ageratum 4. Coleus

- **Cleome** (Cleome hassleriana), also known as Spider Flower.

The spacing between plants should be 12 inches (30 cm).

Cleome tends to get leggy on its lower stems, and other plants should be planted near its base to hide this. The stems are often covered with spines.

- **Coleus** (Solenostemon scutellarioides, Coleus blumei var. verschaffeltii, Coleus x hybridus), Flame Nettle, Painted Nettle, Painted Leaf.

3-inch seedlings need to be pinched for more branching. The spacing between plants should be 8-12 inches (20-30 cm).

- **Cosmos** (Cosmos bipinnatus), also known as Mexican Aster, Cut Leaf Cosmos.

The spacing between plants should be 12-14 inches (30-35 cm). Deadhead to prolong flowering.

- **Dichondra** (Dichondra argentea). This plant is one of the best for hanging baskets. Traditional varieties: "Silver Fall", "Emerald Fall".

- **Gomphrena** (Gomphrena globosa), also known as Globe Amaranth, Globe Flower.

The spacing between plants should be 10-12 inches (25-30 cm).

The floral heads make excellent dried flowers. Only hang them upside down in a well-ventilated place, and you will have color to enjoy all winter.

1. Chinese Aster 2. Cleome 3. Dichondra 4. Cosmos

• **Impatiens** (Impatiens walleriana, Impatiens sultanii or Impatient holstii), also known as Busy Lizzy, Patience Plant, Garden Impatiens, Patient Lucy.

The spacing between plants should be 10-12 inches (25-30 cm).

Don't use this plant on a windy balcony, or protect it from the drought.

• **Lobelia** (Lobelia erinus), also known as Dwarf Annual Lobelia, Edging Lobelia.

The spacing between plants should be 5-6 inches (10-15 cm).

During propagation cut stems on 2-3 inches (5-8 cm) to stimulate new growing and new blooming.

• **Marigold** (Tagetes). We know French (Tagetes patula) and African Marigold (Tagetes erecta).

The spacing between plants should be 10-12 inches (25-30 cm).

• **Morning Glory** (Ipomoea purpurea). Some popular varieties: 'Heavenly Blue', 'Milky Way', 'Scarlet O'Hara', 'Pearly Gates'.

This plant is one of the vines, so needed trellis.

The spacing between plants should be 6-8 inches (15-20 cm).

Soak seeds before sowing in warm water for 24 hours. This plant is not tolerant to transplanting.

1. Gomphrena 2. Lobelia 3. Nasturtium 4. Impatiens

- **Nasturtium** (Tropaeolum majus), also known as Garden Nasturtium, Indian Cress.

The spacing between plants should be 10-12 inches (25-30 cm).

Some varieties of Nasturtium can be used as hanging flowers.

- **Pansy** (Viola x wittrockiana). The spacing between plants should be 5-6 inches (10-15 cm).

Lightly cover the seeds with soil, as they need light to germinate. After sowing, slightly moisten the potting mix and place the seed tray in the refrigerator for two weeks, then move it to heated area. Deadhead to prolong bloom.

- **Petunia** (Petunia grandiflora, Petunia x hybrida, Petunia multiflora). Popular series: 'Dreams', 'Storm', 'Celebrity', 'Duo'; for trailing: 'Wave', 'Rhythm and Blues', 'Spreading Double Wave', 'Shockwave'.

Petunia seeds need addition light for growing, so for beginners it's recommended to buy plants at a local nursery.

Fertilize every two weeks until midsummer. The spacing between plants should be 8-10 inches (20-25 cm).

- **Polka dot plant** (Hypoestes phyllostachya), also known as Hypoestes and Freckle Face.

Pinch back the plants regularly to maintain a bushy growth habit. The spacing between plants should be 10-12 inches (25-30 cm).

1. Morning Glory 2. Petunia 3. Polka-Dot plant 4. Pansy

• **Portulaca** (Portulaca grandiflora), also known as Moss Rose. Some popular varieties: 'Margarita' series, 'Sundial', 'Rio', 'Double', 'Happy Hour'; 'Calypso' mix.

The spacing between plants should be 6-8 inches (15-20 cm).

They do not like transplanting, so handle seedlings carefully. Do not cover the seeds, as light aids germination. Deadhead to reduce self-seeding.

• **Snapdragons** (Antirrhinum majus), also known as Dragon flower.

The spacing between plants should be 10-12 inches (25-30 cm).

[You can read in detail about this plant in my book "Snapdragons: Easy Flower Gardening - Step-By-Step Guide".]

• **Sunflower** (Helianthus annuus). A fascinating variety is 'Chianti Hybrid' with deep wine-red flowers.

Dwarf types (10-24 inches): 'Miss Sunshine', 'Teddy Bear'.

Intermediate types (3-5 feet): 'Sunbright Supreme', 'Sunrich' series, 'Sonya', 'Copper Queen'.

Tall Types (6-12 feet): 'Ring of Fire', 'American Giant Hybrid', 'Skyscraper' (multi-flowered).

The spacing between plants should be 12 inches (30 cm).

• **Sweet peas** (Lathyrus odomtus). The spacing between plants should be 8-10 inches (20-25 cm).

1. Sweet peas, 2. Sunflower, 3. Portulaca, 4. Snapdragons

You should nick your sweet pea seeds before planting or soak them in hot water for a night. This plant grows like a vine, you should think about trellis for it.

During the season you can fertilize your sweet peas three times with any liquid fertilizer.

• **Torenia** (Torenia fournieri), also known as Wishbone Flower.

The spacing between plants should be 5 inches (10 cm). Torenia needs to be protected from the cold wind.

• **Verbena** (Verbena x hybrida). Trailing varieties are great in hanging baskets. It tolerates dry soil.

The spacing between plants should be 8-10 inches (20-25 cm).

Pinch back to keep bushy. Deadhead to prolong bloom.

• **Zinnia** (Zinnia elegans). This plant gives full blooming just in the case it is protected from the wind.
The spacing between plants should be 12-14 inches (30-35 cm).

2.12. Another annuals

You can also use for full sun places Geranium, Pink (Dianthus), Phlox, Aster.

For part-shadow places, you can add Nicotiana, Begonia, and Fuchsia. There you can find a good place for evergreen plants such as Aspidistra, Chloranthus, Privet (Ligustrum).

1. Tagetes 2. Torenia 3. Verbena 4. Zinnia

3. What to Do with the List of Plants

What is the task standing in front of us? We have a balcony or a terrace, small or large it doesn't matter. We have already known our balcony orientation, chosen appropriate plants and learned something about them. What to do next?

You have a lot of time in winter to think about ideas for decorating and arranging of your space. The simplest way is using the web for these purposes.

Many of us are familiar to pinterest.com. Take an hour and spend it viewing pictures there. Type in the search bar "balcony ideas", "terrace flowers", "container gardening" and so on. You will find thousands of ideas.

As for myself, I do so from time to time. It saves time. Of course, I don't repeat exactly what I see, I just capture an idea.

I am searching for something that I like very much. Then I think what was the most attractive to me on that picture. I may like the composition of pots or color scheme. There could be some beautiful flowers or interesting background.

Not so many people can imagine the future result in their mind at first. It's normal, so we should use somebody else's ideas for increasing our imagination and creativity.

When you find a suitable idea you can think about plants and pots.

What supplies do you need to buy?

CONTAINER FLOWER GARDENING

For all varieties of flowers you need:

• Drainage.

This layer is settled on the bottom of the pot. It served for proper watering.

• Soil.

Start with a fresh, sterile mix that will ensure healthy, disease-free seedlings.

• Containers and pots.

You can start seeds in almost any type of containers, as long as it's at least 2-3 inches deep (5-7 cm) and has some drainage holes.

If you are the DIY type, you may want to grow seedlings in milk cartons or paper cups. I prefer the convenience of trays that are made especially for seed starting. It's easy to fill the trays, and I can move them quickly.

• Sprayer (pulverizer) for seedlings.

• Watering-can for adult plants.

• Gloves for working with soil.

• Fertilizers.

You can use any liquid fertilizer for flowering plants. For the majority of annuals, it's not good to use organic food like manure. It consists of huge amount of nitrogen, so your plants will grow very well and have nice, gorgeous foliage, but their blooming will be poor.

• Seeds of chosen flowers.

There is one thing needed to be told. You can buy plants at your local nursery and just transplant them into your containers. It is all you need to do for enjoying their blooming on your balcony.

But buying these plants will probably set you back at least $2-10 per small pot (3-5 plants), whereas a packet of seeds will run you about $4-5 (above 100 seeds). This extra money you may spend on some other gardening supplies.

Even the best garden center doesn't offer some of the most worthy garden annuals, so this is another reason I start annuals from seed myself.

Biennials bloom on the second year of their life, very often in early spring. That's why for these plants it's reasonable to buy them at your local nursery. We are talking about balcony gardening, so I consider that you don't have a free space for growing these plants the whole year without blooming.

3.1. Tips for beginners

The list of flowers from Chapter 2 is very wide. It contains super-easy plants and tricky ones as well. I can recommend for beginners:

▪ Start with hardy flowers and grow them right on your balcony.

▪ Choose flowers with big seeds. They need to be large enough to handle. In this case, you can put each in place easily.

• Don't start with the big amount of different flowers. In the first year, just try to grow a few. You can plant even one species, but in different colors. The goal is to learn and, of course, to achieve the result. Next year you will be much confident and can try more varieties.

• The most easy-growing and easy-care flowers are Tagetes, Cosmos and Snapdragons.

4. How to Grow Annual Plants

The best results you can achieve by growing seedlings. Seedlings of annuals can be transplanted from your apartment to your balcony in the stage of buds. Such plants as viola and petunia can be planted at the stage of blooming.

You can go without seedlings as well. In this case sow your seeds right in the containers.

Annuals started from seeds bloom in this season and produce seeds. In this book, we talk about the best flowers blooming long and plentifully. The majority of them are easy-care. They demonstrate high tolerance to the soil composition and light conditions.

Besides annuals, we may use biennales and perennials for balcony gardening as well. In this case, choose that types which bloom this year.

As I mentioned, there are two ways to start seeds. The first one is planting seeds right in the pots and containers standing outside. The second way consider growing seedlings. Let's investigate these two.

4.1. Growing seedlings

4.1.1. Five steps

Step 1

To start you should prepare your pots and containers – arrange a layer of drainage at the bottom 1-1.5 inches (2-3 cm) and fill them with soil.

After filling your containers, use a small watering can to moisten the planting mix. The goal is to get it moist but not sopping wet. Pack the soil firmly to eliminate gaps.

Remember that most mixes from the shop contain few, if any, nutrients, so you'll need to feed your seedlings with liquid fertilizer a few weeks after they germinate, and continue [every 10-14 days] until you transplant them into the balcony.

Step 2

On the chosen date [we talk about it later] unpack your seeds. The small seeds can be sprinkled right on the soil surface, and then just be powdered with the sand or the soil. Don't make a thick layer as seeds of the majority of annuals need sunlight to germinate.

Larger seeds will need to be buried in ¼ inches (0.5 cm). I plant two seeds per cell (or pot). If both seeds germinate, I snip one and let the other grow.

Step 3

After you've dropped a seed in each cell, you should moisten them. For watering use the sprayer, do it very carefully.

Step 4

To speed germination, cover the pots with plastic wrap or a sheet of glass that fits over the seed-starting tray. It helps keep the seeds moist before they germinate. When you see the first signs of sprouts, you should remove the cover.

Step 5

Put the container on the well-lighted place. It's desirable to use a south windowsill, but you can put your container in any location, but near a window.

If you have the special lightening, you can use it for 4-5 hours a day [on the south window you don't need additional light].

If you're growing under the light, keep in mind that seedlings also need darkness for rest. As soon as the seedlings grow taller, raise the lights.

4.1.2. How to take care of seedlings

As the seedlings grow, use a sprayer or a small watering can to keep the soil moist but not soggy.

Let the soil dry slightly between waterings. Don't open the windows in the room; the temperature should be constant –

in average 66-71 degree F (19-22 °C) [In Chapter 2.6 you can find the germinating temperature for each plant.]

You may set up a fan to ensure good air movement and prevent disease.

Remember to feed the seedlings regularly with liquid fertilizer, mixed at the rate recommended on the package instruction.

Seedlings need a lot of light. Rotate the pots regularly to keep plants from leaning into the light.

4.1.3. How to transplant seedlings outdoors

When the weather outdoors has warmed into the 50 degrees F range (10 °C) at night, you can move your plants outdoors, but do it gradually. It's not a good idea to move your seedlings directly from the protected environment of your home on the balcony or terrace.

You've been coddling these plants for weeks, so they need a gradual transition to the great outdoors. About a week before you are going to set the seedlings into the balcony, place them there for a few hours, bringing them in at night.

Gradually, over the course of a week, expose them to more and more sunshine and the wind. And then finally, your pants will be ready for a set on the open-air permanently.

The final stage is arranging your containers. You need to fill them with the soil as you did before for seed starting. Don't miss a drainage layer. Slightly water the soil. Then make holes in the ground keeping the distances between plants [see Chapter 2.11.]

Select the best seedlings and very carefully transplant them to the new container. Don't try to free their roots; take them with a lump of soil. After transplanting, press the ground around the stem.

4.2. Start seeds right in the pot

Seeds of hardy annuals and biennials can be planted directly in the pots standing on the balcony early in spring. The young plants of hardy annuals tolerate a light frost. They can survive temperature down to 25 degrees F (-5 °C).

Seeds of half-hardy flowers can be planted outdoors too, but you should wait until daytime temperatures outside have risen by 46-50 degrees F (8-10 °C) and the soil has begun to warm up.

Seeds of cold-sensitive plants should be started indoors only if you want to see them bloom.

Looking at the seed packet, you can figure out whether your seeds can be planted right outdoors or not. Usually, it will say something like "direct sow". Also, you can rely on my list from Chapter 2.3.

The time of starting seeds depends on two things:

▪ how long does it take a seed to grow to garden size;

- whether it must wait until after the last frost to live outdoors.

That's why the time of starting seeds is different for each variety of plants.

5 steps for seedlings planting are valid for direct container gardening. When the first sprouts appear, you should remove the cover. From that time, your plants need only regular watering and fertilizing.

When your plants grow taller, you may need to remove excess seedlings. After 1-1.5 months after sowing, the spacing between your plants should be as it was explained in Chapter 2.11.

Don't hurry to throw away excess seedlings. Leave a couple – transplant them somewhere. One or two plants may get sick and die so that some free space will appear. In this case, your saved plants will come in handy.

You should fertilize your plants for prolific blooming. This procedure can take place three times:

- at the age of 10 days

- at the age of 20-30 days.

- a week before blooming.

5. Flowers on the Balcony

The windows and balconies decorated with green plants and flowers look extremely attractive. That is not the only reason why we do balcony gardening. Thick green foliage reduces street noise, clean the air from dust and create cool shade on your terrace.

On the same area (even very small) you can find a place for full sun, part shade and shade-tolerant plants and flowers. Ones can be planted in hanging pots, another settled on the shelves, the other arranged in container and pots at the balcony trellis.

We do not stop at pots and containers choosing, we will move forward. One thing I want to say, "Relay on your taste!" It's reasonable to use the same pots but in different sizes and shapes.

For example, you can buy all the containers made of wood or ceramic. So you can create a monochromatic background and all attention will be paid to your flowers. You can choose plastic pots if you like bright colors. Such choice creates a cheerful atmosphere. Wood and ceramic are more natural materials.

5.1. Arranging plants in the containers

You can arrange your flowers in a large container (10 x 40 inches) depending on their size.

Place the large and tall plants in 1-2 rows per 4 pieces in a row; the medium flowers - in 1-3 rows per 5 items in a row; the short ones – in 3 rows per 7 pieces in a row.

Hanging and small plants are usually put near edges. In this case, their stems will hang out from the container and dramatically decorate it. In the second row, we put medium height flowers.

When our pot is standing near the wall, we can arrange the third row with tall flowers in it or we can plant climbers (vines) there and arrange trellis.

Trellis you can easy do with wooden bars

5.2. Color combinations

As I mentioned before, color combination can be:

• One-color.

• Multicolored.

In the case with flowers, we always deal with at least two colors, because of green (it presents everywhere), but talking about color combinations we consider only colors of flowers.

One-color combination is always good-looking. With multicolored combinations, you should be careful. You can arrange a very harmonious combination, but just adding a wrong color may ruin it.

What do we need to know about colors? It's easy. There are two types – cool and warm colors. Warm ones are red, orange, and yellow. Cool colors are blue, pink, lavender, purple. So you can combine all the warm colors easily together or all the cool colors.

If you want to arrange a container with different flowers, keep in mind that:

• Yellow (warm) looks attractive and bright next to purple (cool).

• Orange (warm) is really good-looking near blue (cool).

• Yellow, orange, red and pink or vinous look harmonious together.

Of course, you can rely on your taste, but think about colors too – this will help you to avoid muddy and inexpressive combinations.

6. Let's Do Together

This final chapter was written for real beginners who have never planted flowers before. I will guide you from the first step to the last one.

I've chosen a photo from the web, as I mentioned for increasing imagination. It is a very simple container we can do together easily.

Our example

6.1. Investigating our example

What have we seen in the picture? Ok, I chose this one because of its bright colors.

I see three verities of flowers obviously. Maybe there are more than three, but we're going to work with three flowers.

At the background, there are snapdragons.

In the middle of the container, we can see tagetes.

And in the front position, we can observe petunias.

Also, I've chosen this picture because I'd known that all three flowers bloom all summer long from June to September.

6.2. What do we need?

I suppose that the container is about 20 inches (50 cm) in diameter. It is round shape. We can use any material; our container can be plastic or ceramic, or made of another material as well.

A few words about seeds. You should buy seeds in a trusted shop. Do it in advance, during winter, for example. You have to be ready for planting in February.

According to petunia's size, I can suppose that tagetes and snapdragons are dwarf.

Thus, we need to buy seeds of Petunia (we see three varieties), dwarf snapdragons (we see the mix) and dwarf tagetes (we see two types). You can buy them all, or rely on your taste.

Also, we need materials from Chapter 3: drainage, soil, etc.

All these plants can be started outdoors, but I don't know your climate zone, so let's grow seedlings. Don't be scared it is easy.

6.3. Let's grow

All our seeds are very small, so be careful with them.

We start seeds on a growing moon. Check the lunar calendar, you can easy find it on-line. We sow the seeds in the first part of February, or in the second depending on when the appropriate phase will be.

Why in February?

Dwarf snapdragons need 70-80 (2.5 months) days after planting to bloom. Tagetes need 45-60 days (1.5-2 months). Petunia needs 80-90 days (2.5-3 months).

We need three pots. In the first one, we sow seeds of Petunia in February; in the second one, we plant seeds of Snapdragons in a month after; in the third one – seeds of Tagetes in 20 days after.

For example:

We choose the date 5, February, 2017. We plant petunia's seeds on this day. Then on 7 or 8 March we sow snapdragon's seeds and on 1-2 April we plant tagetes' seeds.

We do planting in a different time because we want them to bloom together in early June.

Tip!

You can use the information from Chapter 2 and choose those plants which need the same time to bloom. In this case, you have to sow seeds only one time.

How to start seeds you've already known from Chapter 4.

You may ask how many seeds you need to plant. In our example, we can count plant quantity.

We have 3-4 snapdragons, 3-4 tagetes and 3-4 petunias. Double the amount in a case if some seeds won't germinate.

You can plant more seeds, and then do more than one container. Also, you can present extra flowers to your relatives or friends. As you know, flowers are an excellent gift.

Time for transplanting

In the middle of May, we are ready for arranging our balcony container.

Fill it with the soil, moisture it well. Then very carefully transplant your seedlings into it.

Remember, we plant snapdragons on the background. In the middle part of our container, we put tagetes. Petunia is set in the first row.

From this time, our plants need only watering.

How to know if they need water?

It's easy. You should once a day check the soil in the pot with your fingers. If it is dry you should water your plants.

How much water do they need?

Use a small watering can and spill the water slowly. You shouldn't act like you are watering with a hose (we don't have endless earth under our plants). You have to impregnate the soil with water, so if you do it slowly you can stop in the right time.

And one more thing. When the blooming starts you should deadhead your flowers. This procedure prolongs the time of blooming.

At the end of the season, your plants will stop blooming, then turn to yellow and lose their beauty. In that time, you need to throw them away from the pot. The soil may be thrown away too. In this case, you have to use new soil next year.

You can use your old soil if you fertilize it very well. In this situation, next year, before you sow the seeds you should use the fertilizer and add some amount of new soil.

7. Afterward

I hope this book will be helpful for you and you will grow the beautiful flowers.

If you want to know about growing of annuals deeper, you may read my book "Snapdragons: Easy Flower Gardening - Step-By-Step Guide". This book devoted only for one flower, so it has a lot of practical information. Just understand the idea and you will be able to grow almost any annual flower in high professional level.

The book 'The World of Phlox: The Complete Growing Guide: How to Grow and Take Care of Perennial Phlox (Garden Phlox and Creeping Phlox)' may be interesting to those who want to have easy-care perennials in the garden.

If you love the wild styles and natural looks, read the book: 'The Beauty of Prairies: the Secrets of Growing Ornamental Grasses: How to create a natural garden in the wild style of prairies.'

All the books are available on Amazon Kindle.

Thank you very much and I wish you all the best.

Godspeed.

CONTAINER FLOWER GARDENING

40414361R00031

Made in the USA
Middletown, DE
26 March 2019